I want to be a Farmer

I WANT TO BE A
Farmer

DAN LIEBMAN

FIREFLY BOOKS

A Firefly Book

Published by Firefly Books Ltd. 2016

First Printing

Publisher Cataloging-in-Publication Data (U.S.)

Names: Liebman, Daniel, author.
Title: I want to be a farmer / Dan Liebman.
Description: Richmond Hill, Ontario, Canada : Firefly Books, 2016. | Series: I want to be a— | Summary: "A picture book for children who want to know how to become a farmer, what a farmer does, and what makes it fun" -- Provided by publisher.
Identifiers: ISBN 978-1-77085-788-9 (hardcover) | 978-1-77085-787-2 (paperback)
Subjects: LCSH: Farmers — Juvenile literature. | Agriculture – Vocational guidance – Juvenile literature. | Farmers – Vocational guidance – Juvenile literature.
Classification: LCC S494.5.A4L543 |DDC 630.203 – dc23

Library and Archives Canada Cataloguing in Publication

Liebman, Daniel, author
    I want to be a farmer / Dan Liebman.

(I want to be a)
ISBN 978-1-77085-787-2 (paperback).--ISBN 978-1-77085-788-9 (hardback)

    1. Agriculture—Juvenile literature. 2. Farmers—Juvenile literature. I. Title.

S519.L54 2016   j630.2'03   C2016-901037-6

Published in the United States by
Firefly Books (U.S.) Inc.
P.O. Box 1338, Ellicott Station
Buffalo, New York 14205

Published in Canada by
Firefly Books Ltd.
50 Staples Avenue, Unit 1
Richmond Hill, Ontario L4B 0A7

Photo Credits:

© Larry Lefever/Grant Heilman Photography: page 5,

© Images courtesy of the Farm & Food Care Photo Library, Ontario Ministry of Agriculture: pages 6–7, 9, 20

© Terry Brandt/Grant Heilman Photography: page 8

© Dean Rigott/Grant Heilman Photography: page 10

© Jacob Lund/Shutterstock.com: page 11

© Julia Konovalov: page 12, 13, 14, cover

©George Walker/ backcover

© Arthur C. Smith, III/Grant Heilman Photography: page 15

© Lee Snider Photo Images/Shutterstock.com: pages 16-17

© Peter Bernik/Shutterstock.com: page 18

© Pete Burana / Shutterstock.com: page 19

© Production Perig/Shutterstock.com: pages 22, 24

© Fotokostic/Shutterstock.com: page 23

The Publisher acknowledges the financial support for our publishing program by the Government of Canada through the Canada Book Fund as administered by the Department of Canadian Heritage.

Printed in China

Farmers do many different jobs. This boy is feeding a calf on his family's farm.

Animals need attention every day of the week. Farming teaches kids how to care for them.

Some farmers raise cows for milk. Dairy farmers milk their cows two or three times each day.

This farmer is getting ready to harvest pumpkins for Halloween. "Harvesting" means gathering crops from the field.

This farmer grows apples. He is checking the blossoms in the spring. Farmers work every season of the year.

This farmer grows wheat. She is riding on a machine called a "combine." Combines are used to harvest grains.

Farming is a job for the whole family. Children help out when it's feeding time for the goat.

Every morning, before the school bus arrives, this girl gathers eggs from the hens.

This farmer and his son are checking the corn field. Corn is used to make syrup, cereal and, of course, popcorn.

Farmers usually live in a farmhouse on the farm. There are different buildings on a farm.

A silo is a tall, round tower. It is used to store food for farm animals. Many farms have sheds to protect their machines.

If you want to know more about what farmers do, go to a farmer's market in your town or city.

Farmers are all proud of what they do. This man is a coffee bean farmer in Brazil.

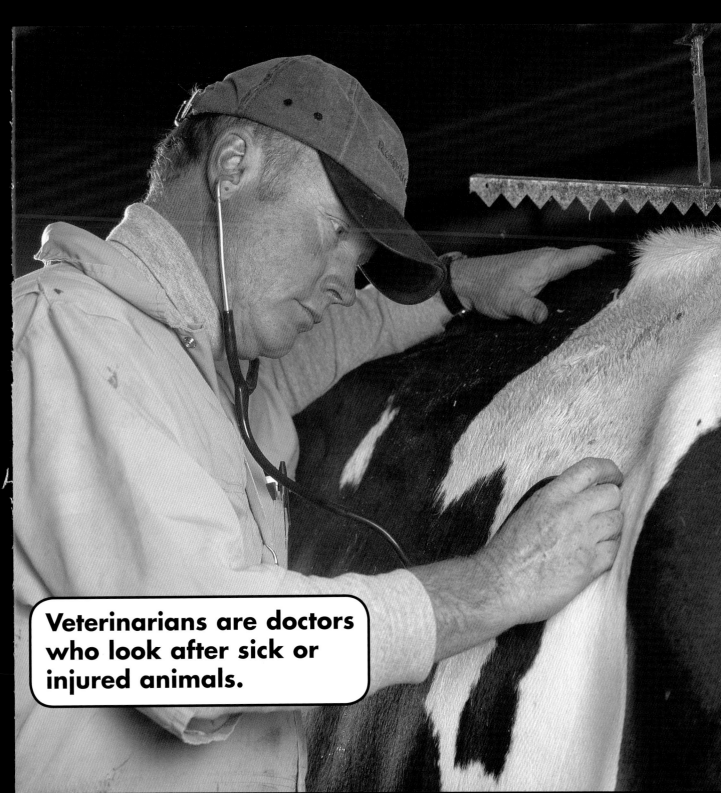

Veterinarians are doctors who look after sick or injured animals.

These farmers grow plants indoors. They use a computer to keep records of the plants.

Farmers work long days. This farmer is plowing the field in the evening. A plow prepares the soil for planting.

Farmers have an important job. Without them, we would not have food to eat.